## Step-by-Step Transformations

# Turning Sand into Glass

**Amy Hayes**

Cavendish Square
New York

Published in 2016 by Cavendish Square Publishing, LLC
243 5th Avenue, Suite 136, New York, NY 10016

Library of Congress Cataloging-in-Publication Data

Hayes, Amy.
Turning sand into glass / Amy Hayes.
pages cm. — (Step-by-step transformations)
Includes index.
ISBN 978-1-50260-452-1 (hardcover) ISBN 978-1-50260-451-4 (paperback) ISBN 978-1-50260-453-8 (ebook)
1. Glass manufacture—Juvenile literature. I. Title.

TP857.3.H39 2016
666'.1—dc23

2015008942


Editorial Director: David MacNamara
Art Director: Jeffrey Talbot
Designer: Alan Sliwinski
Copy Editor: Rebecca Rohan
Senior Production Manager: Jennifer Ryder-Talbot
Production Editor: Renni Johnson
Photo Research by J8 Media

Photos by: Horiyan/Shutterstock.com, cover; Somchai Som/Shutterstock.com, cover; Nomad_Soul/Shutterstock.com, 5; Kris Tripplaar/Sipa USA/Newscom, 7; Joshua Rainey Photography/Shutterstock.com, 9; Per Magnus Persson/Johner Images/Getty Images, 11; AFP/Getty Images, 13; Diyana Dimitrova/Shutterstock.com, 15; Marco Secchi/Getty Images, 17; Carlos Alvarez/Getty Images, 19; Shaun Cammack/E+/Getty Images, 21.

Printed in the United States of America

# Contents

Glass is made from sand.

4

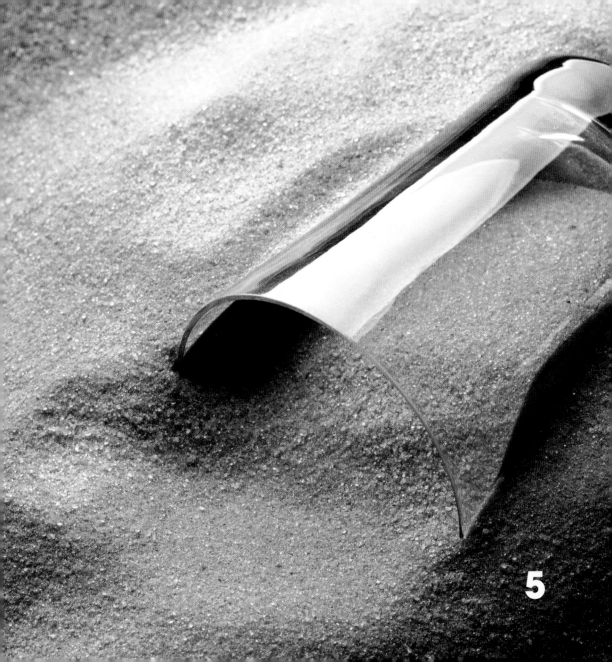

First the sand is put into a **kiln**.

The kiln is very hot.

It melts the sand.

The sand is now a **liquid** glass.

9

Next, a **glassblower** takes the glass out of the kiln.

She uses a long metal **rod** to hold the glass.

The liquid is rolled in blue glass.

This will turn the glass blue.

The glass goes back in the kiln.

13

Next, it is taken out and put into a mold.

The glassblower rolls the glass back and forth.

Then a glassblower blows air through the metal rod.

The air **expands** the glass.

She puts the glass back into the fire to strengthen it.

18

Glass is pretty and useful.

We use glass every day.

**21**

# New Words

**expands** (ex-PANDZ)  Gets bigger.

**glassblower** (GLASS-bloh-er)  Someone who creates art with glass by blowing through a tube.

**liquid** (LIK-kwid)  Flowing freely, not a solid or a gas.

**kiln** (KILN)  An oven that gets very hot.

**rod** (RODD)  Straight, slender metal bar.

# Index

# About the Author

**Amy Hayes** lives in the beautiful city of Buffalo, New York. She has written several books for children, including the Machines that Work and the Step-by-Step Transformations series for Cavendish Square.

## About BOOKWORMS

Bookworms help independent readers gain reading confidence through high-frequency words, simple sentences, and strong picture/text support. Each book explores a concept that helps children relate what they read to the world in which they live.